The
Modern
Rules
of
Order

4th edition

The Modern Rules *of* Order

4th edition

DONALD A. TORTORICE

Printed in the United States of America.

18 17 16 15 14 5 4 3 2 1

Library of Congress Cataloging-in-Publication Data

Tortorice, Donald A.
 The modern rules of order / Donald A. Tortorice. -- 4th edition.
   pages cm
 Includes bibliographical references and index.
 ISBN 978-1-62722-497-0 (alk. paper)
1. Corporate meetings. 2. Business meetings. 3. Meetings. 4. Parliamentary practice. I. Title.
 HD2743.T67 2014
 060.4'2--dc23

                                                        2014000116

Discounts are available for books ordered in bulk. Special consideration is given to state bars, CLE programs, and other bar-related organizations. Inquire at Book Publishing, ABA Publishing, American Bar Association, 321 N. Clark Street, Chicago, Illinois 60654-7598.

www.ShopABA.org

Contents

ABOUT THE AUTHOR

Donald A. Tortorice, Esq., is a member of the American Bar Association and a member of the ABA's Section of Business Law. He has chaired and sat through more business meetings than he cares to remember. A retired partner of the international law firm of Duane Morris, LLP, home based in Philadelphia, he has served as chairman of the Corporation, Banking and Business Law Section of the Pennsylvania Bar Association, president of the Pennsylvania Defense Lawyers Institute, as well as a member of the board of directors of the Pennsylvania Bar Institute, which is the continuing legal education arm of the Pennsylvania Bar Association. He also served as a drafting member of the task force to revise Pennsylvania's corporation and business laws. Mr. Tortorice has sat as a member of the boards of directors of a number of private business corporations and nonprofit organizations.

After retirement from active practice, he became a professor on the faculty at the William & Mary School of Law. In 2009, the graduating class of the law school awarded the Walter L. Williams Prize to Professor Tortorice as their most admired professor. He also served as an adjunct professor of law at the

Dickinson School of Law of the Pennsylvania State University, and as a visiting professor at the law schools of Richmond University and the University of San Diego. He has been a frequent lecturer and course planner in matters relating to business law and administrative law, as well as health and bioethics law. He is the editor of Pennsylvania Business Corporation Practice, the state's foremost corporate practice authority.

Having served as a combat commander of the coastal and river patrol boat in Vietnam, Mr. Tortorice was well prepared for the rigors of legal practice in business law and administrative litigation. He earned his BA with honors from the University of Texas at Austin and his JD from the University of California at Berkeley.

INTRODUCTION

The essential purpose of parliamentary rules for a business meeting is quite simply to provide a framework of established procedures for the orderly and fair conduct of the meeting's business. Procedural rules were never meant to interfere with substantive deliberations of the meeting, but were designed to provide an accepted and understood format for timely consideration and resolution of the meeting's issues.

All too frequently, however, the standard reaction to adopt "traditional parliamentary rules" can lead to confusion, disagreement, and disruption when, in debate on a particularly troublesome issue, it is discovered that the chair of the meeting is not completely familiar with what can be complex and involuted procedures required by traditional rules. This is not surprising since traditional rules were tailored to formally structured parliamentary debate. It is significant to note that Clarence Cannon, former parliamentarian of the U.S. House of Representatives, wrote that complex rules of order are not appropriate for small assemblies or business meetings:

These rules of Parliament and Congress are designed

for bicameral bodies, generally with paid memberships, meeting in continuous session, requiring a majority for a quorum, and delegating their duties largely to committees. Their special requirements . . . have produced highly complex and remarkably efficient systems of rules peculiar to their bodies, but which are, as a whole, unsuited to the needs of the ordinary assembly.

Rules of parliamentary procedure stemming from *Robert's Rules* are neither appropriate for nor applicable to the corporate or nonprofit business meeting. State laws and corporate bylaws are generally silent regarding the procedural conduct of meetings, and there are no other detailed procedural rules for business meetings that are commonly accepted.

The objective of *The Modern Rules of Order* is to provide a more modern and simplified procedure that promotes efficiency, decorum and fairness in a form that can be easily mastered and later referred to with ease. They are designed for application to a business meeting, whether the business is that of a major corporation or a small nonprofit association. The focus is upon promoting timely consideration of the substance of the meeting rather than ritualistic procedure.

Significant authority is given to the chair, whose judgment should be respected by the meeting and who will conduct matters in the best interests of the organization. This is the case in the vast majority of meetings convened every day. Where it is not true, remedial action may be appropriate to restore effective leadership. Procedural measures are no substitute for this. The essential requirements for the procedural framework of any meeting, as stated in judicial precedent, is that the meeting be conducted with fairness and good faith toward all who are entitled to take part, and that those present be given an opportunity to consider and act upon matters properly brought before the meeting.

SAMPLE BYLAW OR RESOLUTION ADOPTING THESE RULES

Meetings of the [members/board of directors/stockholders*] of this [corporation/association*] shall be conducted according to the Modern Rules of Order.

   *Select whichever is applicable.

The essence of this book is embodied in only two mandatory rules. They are as follows:

Rule 1

Role of the Chair

Authority for conduct of the meeting shall be assigned to the chair, who shall be responsible for timely, fair, and reasonable conduct of the meeting's business. Decisions of the chair are final on questions of procedure, except that any ruling may be appealed to a vote of the meeting. If a ruling of the chair is corrected by the meeting, the chair shall amend its ruling to reflect the will of the meeting.

Rule 2

The Rules and Governing Law

The rules of conduct of the meeting are subordinate to bylaws of the organization, which are subordinate to the articles (or charter) and to prevailing state or federal law.

All other rules set forth and discussed in this book are simply guidance to the chair and are subject to Rules 1 and 2.

RULES OF ORDER

Rules 1 and 2 are mandatory; the remaining rules serve as guidance to the chair and are subject to Rules 1 and 2.

Rule 1

Role of the Chair

Authority for conduct of the meeting shall be assigned to the chair, who shall be responsible for timely, fair, and reasonable conduct of the meeting's business. Decisions of the chair are final on questions of procedure, except that any ruling may be appealed to a vote of the meeting. If a ruling of the chair is corrected by the meeting, the chair shall amend its ruling to reflect the will of the meeting.

Rule 2

The Rules and Governing Law

The rules of conduct of the meeting are subordinate to bylaws of the organization, which are subordinate to the articles (or charter) and to prevailing state or federal law.

Rule 3

The Agenda

The chair shall be responsible for establishing the order of business, or agenda, in consultation with the secretary, and shall ensure that the order of business is posted or circulated as required by the bylaws, articles, or law.

Rule 4

Convening the Meeting

The chair shall be responsible for ascertaining and announcing the presence of a quorum and the due convening of the meeting.

Rule 5

Special Officers

The chair shall have authority to appoint a special chair to conduct the meeting, a special secretary to record minutes, or other special officers for the purpose of assisting in conduct of the meeting. The special chair or other specially appointed officers shall serve under the authority of and be subject to direction of the elected chair. A special secretary shall also serve under supervision of the elected secretary.

Rule 6

Approval of Minutes and Reports as Submitted

By announcement of the chair, unless an objection is raised, previously circulated minutes of meetings and reports not requiring action may be approved as submitted. If an objection is made, approval shall be presented in the form of a motion.

Rule 7

General Discussion

Issues that require consideration of the meeting may be discussed with or without formal motion. An issue may be resolved (a) by recording the general consensus or "sense of the meeting" or (b) by a formal motion.

Rule 8

General Principles for Discussion or Debate

Discussion of any issue is subject to regulation by the chair to assure adequate consideration of relevant points of view in the best interests of the organization. The objectives of discussion are:

    (a) to determine the will of the body and to articulate decisions for conduct of business;

    (b) to assure sufficient discussion and consideration of issues so that all pertinent points of view are considered;

    (c) to maintain at all times the dignity of the meeting so that each recognized speaker's views are made known to voting participants and to ensure that appropriate respect is accorded all members; and

    (d) to present the consideration of business in a manner understood by all participants.

Rule 9

General Consensus or Sense of the Meeting

When a course of action is embraced by a clear consensus of meeting participants, the chair may, if there is no objection, state that action upon the issue is resolved by "general consensus" or the "sense of the meeting." A ruling as to general consensus or the sense of the meeting shall be recorded in the minutes as the decision of the meeting.

Rule 10

Use of Motion Practice

Where a sense of the meeting cannot be determined with reasonable certainty (as discussed in Rule 9), or where by reason of importance of the matter formal approval or a count of the votes is desired, the chair or any member may state the proposal as a motion governed by motion practice as set forth in Rule 12.

Rule 11

Motion Practice

The rules of motion practice shall be applied as a guide to the chair in disposition of formal motions, which are resolved by a vote of the meeting.

Rule 12

Motion Practice and Precedence

Under these rules, motions should be limited to those set forth below. They are grouped into three categories and listed in order of precedence; when any motion is pending, any motion listed above it in the list is in order, but those below it are out of order.

Where a required vote is stated, reference is made to those present and voting or, in situations such as shareholders meetings where participants may have more than one vote, reference is to the number of votes cast.

MEETING CONDUCT MOTIONS.

1. Point of Privilege.

   Characteristics:

   - May interrupt a speaker.
   - Second not required.
   - Not debatable.
   - Not amendable.
   - Resolved by the chair, no vote is required.

2. Point of Procedure.

   Characteristics:

   - May interrupt a speaker.
   - Second not required.
   - Not debatable.
   - Not amendable.

- Resolved by the chair; no vote is required.

Similar Motions Included: Point of order, point of inquiry.

3. To Appeal a Ruling of the chair.

Characteristics:
- May not interrupt a speaker.
- Second required.
- Debatable.
- Not amendable.
- Majority vote required.

Special Note: If a ruling of the chair is based upon governing law (e.g., not a proper subject of the meeting or a matter requiring prior notice), it is not appealable.

4. To Recess the Meeting.

Characteristics:
- May not interrupt a speaker.
- Second required.
- Debatable.
- Amendable.
- Majority vote required.

DISPOSITION MOTIONS.

1. To Withdraw a Motion.

Characteristics:
- May interrupt a speaker.
- Second not required.

- Not debatable.
- Not amendable.
- Resolved by the chair, no vote is required.

2. To Postpone Consideration.

   Characteristics:

   - May not interrupt a speaker.
   - Second required.
   - Debatable.
   - Amendable.
   - Majority vote required.

   Similar Motion Included: To table; to postpone indefinitely.

3. To Refer.

   Characteristics:

   - May not interrupt a speaker.
   - Second required.
   - Debatable
   - Amendable.
   - Majority vote required.

4. To Amend.

   Characteristics:

   - May not interrupt a speaker.
   - Second required.
   - Debatable.
   - Amendable.
   - Majority vote required.

5. To Limit, Extend, or Close Debate.

   Characteristics:

   - May not interrupt a speaker.
   - Second required.
   - Debatable.
   - Amendable.
   - Two-thirds vote required.

   Similar Motions Included: To move the question; to call the previous question.

6. To Count the Vote.

   Characteristics:

   - May not interrupt a speaker.
   - Second required.
   - Not debatable.
   - Not amendable.
   - Mandatory when seconded; no vote required.

   Similar Motions Included: To divide the assembly.

MAIN MOTIONS—TO TAKE ACTION OR RECONSIDER ACTION TAKEN.

   Characteristics:

   - May not interrupt a speaker.
   - Second required.
   - Debatable.
   - Amendable.

- Majority vote required unless a greater vote is prescribed by the bylaws, articles, or law.

Rule 13

Elections

Elections are initiated by the process of nomination set forth in the bylaws, charter, or prevailing law. If more than one candidate is nominated to any office, reasonable discussion should be allowed as to the fitness of candidates to serve. For particular offices, a majority vote is required; however, the directors are chosen by plurality vote (unless otherwise prescribed in the bylaws, charter, or governing law).

Rule 14

Adjournment

Upon completion of the meeting's agenda, if no further business is indicated, the chair shall adjourn the meeting. Adjournment may be accomplished by motion or announcement of the chair. A motion to adjourn prior to completion of the agenda is out of order.

Rule 15

Minutes

Minutes of the meeting shall be recorded by or under supervision of the secretary and be submitted for approval at a subsequent meeting. In the absence of the secretary, the chair shall appoint a special secretary of the meeting.

CHART OF GUIDANCE FOR MOTION PRACTICE

Motion	Interrupt a Speaker?	Second Required?	Debatable?	Amendable?	Vote Required?
MEETING CONDUCT MOTIONS:					
Point of Privilege	yes	no	no	no	none
Point of Procedure	yes	no	no	no	none
To Appeal	no	yes	yes	no	majority
To Recess	no	yes	yes	yes	majority
DISPOSITION MOTIONS:					
To Withdraw	yes	no	no	no	none
To Postpone Consideration	no	yes	yes	yes	majority
To Refer	no	yes	yes	yes	majority
To Amend	no	yes	yes	yes	majority
To Limit, Extend, or Close Debate	no	yes	yes	yes	2/3
To Count the Vote	no	yes	no	no	none
MAIN MOTIONS:					
To Take Action, To Reconsider, or To Elect	no	yes	yes	yes	majority unless otherwise required

DISCUSSION OF THE RULES

Rule 1

Role of the Chair

Authority for conduct of the meeting is assigned to the chair, who shall be responsible for timely, fair, and reasonable conduct of the meeting's business. Decisions of the chair are final on questions of procedure, except that any ruling may be appealed to a vote of the meeting. If a ruling of the chair is corrected by the meeting, the chair shall amend its ruling to reflect the will of the meeting.

There must be a central authority for conduct of the meeting. The logical person to assume that authority is the elected chief executive officer (CEO) who, under most bylaws, is charged with responsibility for conducting meetings of stockholders (members) or the board. As the highest elected official of the organization, the CEO should have the confidence of the board, the officers, and stockholders (members). If the meeting is a body other than the board (a committee, for example), the rules apply equally to that body and its appointed or elected Chair.

A principal element of these rules is to place in the hands of the chair the requisite authority to lead the meeting through its business, using these rules as a guide. To impose upon the chair a set of complex and unyielding strictures, frequently diverting the meeting from focused attention to business, has the untoward result of turning the meeting inside out, with emphasis upon form rather than substance, procedure rather than business.

The purpose of these rules is to emphasize substance over form, under the leadership and control of the elected Chair. However, the essential element of democratic form is preserved through the right of any member to appeal a ruling of the chair to the meeting as a whole. If this approach does not work, the fault may lie not in the inadequacy of rules but in a lack of effective leadership. However, the vast majority of organizations that turn to these rules will find that they enhance the guidance of capable leaders within a setting of logical and streamlined procedure that restores emphasis on attention to business.

Rule 2

The Rules and Governing Law
The rules of conduct of the meeting are subordinate to

bylaws of the organization, which are subordinate to the articles (or charter) and to prevailing state or federal law.

This rule simply recites the existing priority of governing law. Prevailing federal or state law is the highest regulatory authority under which all organizations must operate. Under the law, the articles or charter of the organization are the most fundamental internal governing mandate, complemented by the bylaws, a more expansive and detailed set of voluntary regulations. Meetings governed by these rules will always be subject to bylaws of the organization, which must be compatible with the articles or charter, which, in turn, cannot violate substantive state or federal law.

Rule 3

The Agenda

The chair shall be responsible for establishing the order of business, or agenda, in consultation with the secretary, and shall ensure that the order of business is posted or circulated as required by the bylaws, articles, or law.

A written agenda, distributed beforehand, is usually advisable for all meetings, whether general or special. The agenda, or order of business, sets forth the order and scope of issues to be resolved. Preparation of a formal agenda is not mandatory, although the general rule governing special meetings is that the meeting may address only those items that are appropriately stated in the call of the meeting. In addition, certain matters, typically amendments to organizational documents, must be circulated to members beforehand in order to be legally placed before the meeting. It is therefore always advisable, in advance of a meeting, to review matters to be presented so that special notice requirements are satisfied.

Rule 4

Convening the Meeting

The chair shall be responsible for ascertaining and announcing the presence of a quorum and the due convening of the meeting.

The chair's first duty is to call the assembled members of the meeting to order.

The chair shall then announce, having ascertained beforehand, that a quorum is present and that the meeting is ready to proceed with its business. Once a quorum is established, the meeting can continue to transact business until adjournment, even if departure of members leaves less than the original quorum.

If a quorum is not present when the meeting is convened, the chair must announce that fact and adjourn the meeting, whether for minutes or for days, until a quorum is assembled. If, pending the appearance of a quorum, the meeting should proceed with discussion or action, it is essential to understand that any decisions made at the meeting are advisory and without authority of the body unless they are subsequently adopted by a meeting having a quorum present.

Rule 5

Special Officers

The chair shall have authority to appoint a special chair to conduct the meeting, a special secretary to record minutes, or other special officers for the purpose of assisting in conduct of the meeting. The special chair or other specially appointed officers shall serve under the authority of and be subject to direction of the elected chair. A special secretary shall also serve under supervision of the elected secretary.

Having convened the meeting, the chair has authority to appoint a special chair, if desired. This appointment does not in any way diminish the elected chair's responsibility or authority for conduct of the meeting, but simply enables an elected chair, who may be inexperienced or otherwise disinclined to govern the meeting, to appoint an individual to serve in the chair's stead. Similarly, the chair may appoint a special secretary upon the advice of the elected secretary, but again, that appointment is subject to the supervision and ultimate authority of the elected secretary.

Rule 6

Approval of Minutes and Reports as Submitted

By announcement of the chair, unless an objection is raised, previously circulated minutes of meetings and reports not requiring action may be approved as submitted. If an objection is made, approval shall be presented in the form of a motion.

If the minutes of a prior meeting have been circulated, the chair should simply ask if there are corrections. If the minutes have not been circulated, the secretary should read the minutes and corrections should be taken. Following notation of corrections, the chair should announce that the minutes as circulated (or as corrected) stand approved. If there is dispute on a correction, the proposed correction should be put in the form of a main motion, discussed, and voted upon, with the ultimate decision representing the final record of the meeting.

The chair shall, as appropriate, call upon officers and

committee chairs to deliver reports of studies undertaken or action recommended. Following each report, the chair may ask for a motion of approval or may simply state that, without objection, the report stands approved.

Rule 7

General Discussion

Issues that require consideration of the meeting may be discussed with or without formal motion. An issue may be resolved (a) by recording the general consensus or "sense of the meeting" or (b) by a formal motion.

This rule, which provides that issues requiring consideration of the meeting may be discussed with or without formal motion, reflects the current practice of most business meetings. Once an issue has been stated by the chair, by report of a committee, or otherwise, the issue may be discussed generally in the absence of a formal motion. Frequently, the best interests of the organization will become easily distilled such that a general consensus can be determined. If the issue cannot be resolved by consensus, the chair should call for a formal motion.

Rule 8

General Principles for Discussion or Debate

Discussion of any issue is subject to regulation by the chair to assure adequate consideration of relevant points of view in the best interests of the organization. The objectives of discussion are:

(a) to determine the will of the body and to articulate decisions for conduct of business;

(b) to assure sufficient discussion and consideration of issues so that all pertinent points of view are considered;

(c) to maintain at all times the dignity of the meeting so that each recognized speaker's views are made known to voting participants and to ensure that appropriate respect is accorded all members; and

(d) to present the consideration of business in a manner understood by all participants.

This rule recites the fundamental objectives for any business discussion. Obviously, the essential goal is to determine the will of the meeting and to articulate decisions so that conduct of the organization's business may proceed in accord with those decisions. In arriving at conclusions, sufficient discussion and consideration of issues must be allowed so that all pertinent points of view are considered. Prudent leadership requires that the meeting hear all points of view, and molding different approaches or opinions into a general consensus is the hallmark of capable leadership.

The right to speak should be accorded to one speaker at a time, whose comments, subject to reasonable time limitation, should be heard without interruption, except for certain privileged motions noted in Rule 12, Motion Practice and Precedence.

The dignity of the meeting must always be preserved so that appropriate respect is accorded all members. Personal invective, inappropriate language, or churlish conduct should not be tolerated and must be ruled out of order whenever it occurs, or upon the raising of a point of privilege. Finally, it is essential that in arriving at a decision, whether it be the statement of the sense of the meeting or the wording of a motion, the proposal should be written down and stated clearly so that the proposal under consideration is known to all participants.

Rule 9

General Consensus or the Sense of the Meeting
When a course of action is embraced by a clear consensus of meeting participants, the chair may, if there is no

objection, state that action upon the issue is resolved by "general consensus" or the "sense of the meeting." A ruling as to general consensus or the sense of the meeting shall be recorded in the minutes as the decision of the meeting.

Following discussion of an issue, common sense and necessity, together with appropriate business judgment, usually lead to a course of action that meets the approval of meeting participants. When it is clear to the chair that there is a genuine sense of the meeting as to action to be taken, the issue may be simply resolved by the chair stating, "Without objection, the sense of the meeting is that . . . ." This statement, with no objection raised, is recorded in the minutes and becomes the decision of the meeting.

Rule 10

Usage of Motion Practice

Where a sense of the meeting cannot be determined with reasonable certainty (as discussed in Rule 9), or where by reason of importance of the matter formal approval or a count of the votes is desired, the chair or any member may state the proposal as a motion governed by motion practice as set forth in Rule 12.

Whenever the chair realizes there is a significant division within the meeting or that a reliable sense of the meeting cannot be stated, a motion should be invited that will bring about formal resolution by discussion leading to a vote of the meeting. It is also the right of any member, at any time during discussion, to propose resolution of an issue by motion. When seconded, that motion becomes the issue under consideration, subject to debate, amendment, and final disposition by vote of the meeting.

Rules 11 and 12

Motion Practice and Precedence

The rules of motion practice shall be applied as a guide to the chair in disposition of formal motions, which are resolved by a vote of the meeting.

Under these rules, motions should be limited to those set forth below. They are grouped into three categories and listed in order of precedence; when any motion is pending, any motion listed above it in the list is in order, but those below it are out of order.

Where a required vote is stated, reference is made to those present and voting or, in situations such as shareholders' meetings where participants may have more than one vote, reference is to the number of votes cast.

All essential motions can be grouped into three categories:

(a) meeting conduct motions that relate to how the meeting shall proceed,

(b) disposition motions that are subordinate to but affect or dispose of main motions, and

(c) main motions.

Meeting conduct motions carry a sense of urgency. Therefore they are the most privileged and have the highest priority for action. Main motions are the fundamental issues facing the meeting for decision. In the usual circumstance, only one main motion should be considered at a time; each should be resolved before the meeting proceeds to the next issue. Because disposition motions affect main motions, they logically have precedence over main motions and therefore may be raised while main motions are pending.

The rules set forth the general precedence of motions and act as a guide to the chair. If circumstances call for a departure from stated procedure, however, it is within the general authority of the chair to determine conduct of the meeting, subject to appeal.

The principal motions necessary for motion practice are discussed below.

Point of Privilege—A point of privilege, sometimes called a point of personal privilege, is a communication from a member to the chair, drawing urgent attention to a need for personal accommodation. For example, the point may relate to an inability to see or hear, a matter of comfort, a matter of requested convenience, or an overlooked right or privilege that should have been accorded. In essence, it is a call to the chair for the purpose of assuring a member's convenient and appropriate participation in the meeting.

Because of its urgent nature, a point of privilege may interrupt a speaker. Because it is addressed to the attention and action of the chair, it may not be debated or amended, and no vote is required.

Point of Procedure—A point of procedure, often called a point of order, is a question addressed to the chair, either inquiring into the manner of conducting business or raising a question about the propriety of a particular procedure. It is simply an inquiry and is resolved by correction or clarification by the chair.

A point of procedure may interrupt a speaker. Because it is addressed to action by the chair, a second is not required. It should not be debated or amended.

To Appeal a Ruling of the Chair—The rules provide that decisions or rulings of the chair are final on questions of procedure, except that the chair's ruling may be appealed to a vote of the meeting. Whenever a member questions the appropriateness or essential fairness of the chair's ruling, that member may appeal the ruling to a vote of the meeting. However, if a motion is out of order as a matter of law (not a proper subject of the meeting, improper notice given, etc.), the chair's ruling is not appealable.

A motion to appeal may not interrupt a speaker. In order to prevent frivolous appeals, a second is required. The motion is subject to debate, which should be brief, and by its nature, is not amendable. In order to overrule a procedural decision of the chair, a majority vote is required.

To Recess the Meeting—A motion to recess requests a brief interruption of the meeting's business, usually so that some ancillary matter may be addressed, or simply to provide a needed break. Unless stated in the motion, the period of recess shall be decided by the chair. If necessary, a recess may extend the meeting from one day to another.

The motion may not interrupt a speaker, and a second is required. It is debatable. It may be amended, and a majority vote is required.

To Withdraw a Motion—A motion to withdraw may be made only by the maker of the motion and is essentially a communication to the chair that the maker is withdrawing the proposal. This is the maker's privilege; thus, it does not require a second. In addition, because a similar motion can be made later by another member, a withdrawal should not be subject to debate, amendment, or vote. The chair should simply state that the motion is withdrawn, and the meeting should proceed with a new treatment of the issue at hand—or a new issue.

Because the motion obviates discussion, it may interrupt a speaker.

To Postpone Consideration—This motion may arise from a need for further information, a matter of convenience, or for any other reason that will enable the meeting to deal with the issue more effectively at a later time. The motion includes traditional motions to table or to postpone indefinitely—motions usually proposed to defeat an issue. Unless otherwise specifically provided in the motion itself, a postponed motion may be renewed at a later appropriate time.

The motion may not interrupt a speaker; requires a second; is debatable; and is amendable, particularly as to postponement timing. A majority vote is required.

To Refer—A motion to refer is typically used to submit an issue to a committee, usually for study leading to a subsequent recommendation. Because it ordinarily disposes the motion for purposes of the current meeting, a motion to refer is subject to the same rules that apply to the main motion.

It may not interrupt a speaker, a second is required, it is debatable and amendable, and a majority vote is required.

To Amend—A motion to amend proposes a change in the

wording of a motion currently under consideration. When a motion to amend is pending and an amendment to the amendment is proposed, the chair should focus discussion on the latest amendment, resolve that question, then proceed to the first amendment before continuing discussion on the main motion. Votes on amendments are thus in reverse order of the sequence in which they are proposed.

A motion to amend may not interrupt a speaker, requires a second, and is debatable and amendable. A majority vote is required for approval of the amendment. It should also be noted that governing law often restricts amendments to proposals that are required to be set forth in the notice of the meeting such that they may not enlarge the original purpose of the proposal.

To Limit, Extend, or Close Debate—Because the extent to which an issue is discussed rests primarily with discretion of the chair, it is the chair who carries the burden of ensuring that adequate exposure is given to differing points of view. A motion to limit, extend, or close debate is therefore an overruling of the chair's determination. A motion to close debate is the same as a motion to move the question or to call the previous question.

Because this motion affects the most fundamental right of any member, the right to speak one's views, it is the only procedural motion that requires greater than a majority vote—a two-thirds vote of participants voting is required.

To Count the Vote—A motion to count the vote should be limited to those circumstances where the convenient hearing of "yeas" and "nays" cannot clearly resolve the issue. It represents the right of a member to have a vote demonstrated by count. That count may be directed by the chair either as a showing of hands or a standing of voting members while the vote is recorded. Upon completion of the count, the chair announces the result—and final disposition of the issue voted upon. This motion is the same as the antiquated "motion for division of the assembly."

It may not interrupt a speaker, requires a second, is neither debatable nor amendable, and because of the importance of the matter, should be considered mandatory, and thus no vote is required.

Main Motions—A main motion states proposed policy or action on a substantive issue considered by the body. As such, it may be an initial call to take particular action, to reconsider action taken, to rescind a prior decision, or to elect persons to office. Although lowest in precedence among all motions, main motions are clearly the most important: through their content, the business decisions of the body are determined.

A main motion may be made only when a prior main motion has been disposed of. It may not interrupt a speaker, a second is required, it is debatable and amendable, and a majority vote is required unless a greater vote is prescribed by the bylaws, articles, or governing law.

Unnecessary Motions

There are a number of archaic or simply unnecessary motions that complicate and encumber procedure without adding clarity, fairness, or efficiency in the conduct of business. The substance of these motions may be incorporated into recognized motions or may otherwise be handled effectively by the chair's direction of the meeting through its business. Such motions are as follows:

To Suspend the Rules—This is traditionally a motion to violate established rules, due usually to circumstances that require taking a matter out of order or hearing a point of view on a matter that has been closed. Such circumstances should be left to the discretion of the chair in permitting or denying the requested action. In the vast majority of circumstances, resolution of the matter will be an obvious exercise of common sense by the chair.

To Convene a Committee of the Whole—This motion usually seeks to avoid particular rules that apply to the entire meeting but not to committee deliberations. Under these rules, no such distinction exists.

To Table—The purpose of a motion to table is either to postpone consideration of a motion, which is treated by a motion to postpone, or to defeat a motion, which is realized by the meeting's ultimate disposition of the issue. It should be treated as a motion to postpone.

To Move (or Call) the Question—This is essentially a motion to close debate. It is a call to the chair to move to an expeditious vote on the matter. Such a decision rests with the chair, subject to a motion to close debate. It is an unnecessary motion since at any point during discussion, a speaker may suggest that the issue has been adequately discussed and request that the chair bring the matter to resolution. Unless relevant points of view have not been heard, a positive response from the chair usually follows.

To Move a Point of Parliamentary Inquiry—Such a motion should be treated as a point of procedure. The mover should put the inquiry in the form of a question addressed to the chair. The chair will respond, and the meeting will proceed.

To Object to Consideration—This arcane motion is really an expression of disfavor with the issue being presented and should be treated as a point of procedure to be resolved by the chair.

To Make an Order of the Day, General or Special—In business meetings, general or special "orders of the day" are wholly unnecessary. General orders usually are set on the agenda as unfinished business, and new orders may be raised as new business. In any event, any issue that a member believes should be brought before the meeting can be posed in response to a call for new business.

To Divide a Question—A motion for division of a question can be considered as either a request to the chair to separate a motion containing different elements into separate motions, or it may be considered an amendment. Such matters should be handled by the chair, who, if the current main motion is complex, may divide it into its separate components. Otherwise, the motion to divide should be considered a motion to amend.

Rule 13

Elections

Elections are initiated by the process of nomination set forth in the bylaws, charter, or prevailing law. If more than one candidate is nominated to any office, reasonable discussion should be allowed as to the fitness of candidates to serve. For particular offices, a majority vote is required; however, the directors are chosen by plurality vote (unless otherwise prescribed in the bylaws, charter, or governing law).

Elections are accomplished by nomination and voting procedures set forth usually in governing law, often amplified by provisions of the organization's charter or bylaws.

If there is only one candidate for each position, then a motion to elect such candidate (or slate of candidates) unanimously, or by acclamation, is in order.

If there is no bylaw requiring nominations to be submitted prior to the meeting, nominations are made from the floor and a second to each nomination should be required. Reasonable discussion should be allowed concerning qualification of nominees.

Where an election is to fill a particular office, the choice should be by majority vote. If there are more than two candidates and no candidate receives a majority on the first vote, then a second vote should be taken among those candidates who received the highest number of votes.

Where a body of specified number, such as a board of directors, is being elected and there are more candidates than the number of positions to be filled, those receiving the largest number of votes, even if less than a majority, are elected.

Unless otherwise provided:

- ballots may be used but are not necessary;
- members do not have a right to a secret ballot;
- on a vote taken by voice vote or a raising of hands, the ruling of the chair is binding unless there is an appropriate motion to count the vote;
- where voting is not on a per-person basis, such as a voting by shares, and a voice vote is inappropriate, balloting is ordinarily necessary; and
- judges of election may be appointed to determine the rights of members to vote and to determine the results of voting.

Rule 14

Adjournment

Upon completion of the meeting's agenda, if no further business is indicated, the chair shall adjourn the meeting. Adjournment may be accomplished by motion or announcement of the chair. A motion to adjourn prior to completion of the agenda is out of order.

A motion to adjourn may be made only at the invitation of the chair when scheduled agenda items have been completed. At any other time, the motion is out of order. The motion may not interrupt a speaker and no second is required. The motion is debatable, at least to the extent of setting a time for reconvening if an announcement to this effect has not already been made.

The chair has the discretion of calling for a vote to adjourn, or may simply declare, without objection, that the meeting is adjourned.

Rule 15

Minutes

Minutes of the meeting shall be recorded by or under supervision of the secretary and be submitted for approval at a subsequent meeting. In the absence of the secretary, the chair shall appoint a special secretary of the meeting.

Minutes are discussed in Chapter Four.

TYPICAL MEETING AGENDAS

The following are typical agendas for an annual general meeting of stockholders (or members) and a regular meeting of directors.

ANNUAL MEETING OF STOCKHOLDERS OR MEMBERS

AGENDA

1. Call to order and establishment of a quorum
2. Introductions (directors, officers, auditors, counsel, visitors)
3. Presentation of meeting notice, stockholder (or member) list, and meeting agenda
4. Appointments or elections for the meeting
   a. Special chair or secretary, if appropriate
   b. Judges of election or other special officers
5. Reports
   a. Officers

          i.   Treasurer

          ii.   President

          iii.   Others

    b.   Standing committees

    c.   Special committees

6. Election of directors

    a.   Nominations and/or report of nominating committee

    b.   Discussion of candidates

    c.   Casting of votes

    d.   Report of judges of election

7. Unfinished business

8. New business

9. Adjournment

MEETING OF DIRECTORS

AGENDA

1. Establishment of a quorum

2. Appointments for the meeting

    a.   Special chair, if appropriate

    b.   Special secretary, if appropriate

3. Approval of prior minutes

4. Elections

5. Reports

    a.   Officers

      i.   Treasurer

      ii.   President

      iii. Others

   b.   Standing committees

   c.   Special committees

6. Unfinished business

7. Appointment of committees

8. New business

9. Adjournment

DISCUSSION OF MINUTES, AND GENERAL GUIDELINES FOR THE CONDUCT OF MEETINGS

Chapter Four

Approval of Minutes

Approved minutes of a meeting become the official record of policies adopted or actions taken. In addition to providing a permanent record, they are the definitive source upon which the organization relies for authorizing policy or action.

A record of each meeting is made by the secretary or a special secretary, if appointed. When transcribed into minutes, the notes become a tentative record of the meeting, and are submitted for approval usually at the next meeting. (However, where a motion is submitted in writing or a proposal is set forth in full in a notice of the meeting, the minutes containing the text of the proposal

41

are definitive immediately and may be relied upon as action of the organization.) Any record made by a special secretary is subject to the control and supervision of the elected secretary, who has formal responsibility to prepare and maintain the organization's records. Minutes should be sent to members prior to the following meeting so that they may be reviewed for accuracy and completeness without requiring a full line-by-line reading at the meeting. Minutes that have not been circulated beforehand should be read before approval is requested. Also, if minutes have not been circulated, it is possible to postpone approval until a later meeting, thereby allowing circulation beforehand. However, a regular practice of postponing approval should be avoided because delay makes the process of approval or correction more difficult.

Minutes of shareholder or member meetings may be approved by the directors.

When minutes are presented for approval, the chair should request corrections. If there are none, the chair may simply announce that the minutes have been approved as submitted. If a correction is noted and accepted by all members, the chair will announce that the minutes shall be corrected as noted. Annotation of the correction is made on the face of the minutes and the fact that a correction has been made is set forth in the minutes of the current meeting. If there is disagreement with respect to a correction, the chair should invite the member proposing the correction to state the correction as a motion, which is followed by brief discussion, possible amendment, and a vote of the meeting. Minutes approved by the meeting thus become the official record of the body.

Content of Minutes

Minutes vary significantly from organization to organization in style and content. There is no one correct form. The essential requirement is that minutes contain a record of official policy adopted or action authorized. They need not be an exhaustive record of deliberation.

The first paragraph should recite the nature of the meeting, where it was held, the date and time of convening, and state what notice was given. It should then name the presiding chair and recording secretary.

The next note typically is that the meeting was called to order and a quorum was present. For all but regularly scheduled meetings, the minutes should contain a statement relating to notice or call of the meeting and, in the case of annual meetings, should record other pre-meeting communication such as mailing of proxy solicitations or annual reports.

After confirmation of notice, the chair should either make appointments of special officers for the meeting, such as tellers or judges of election, or note that such appointments have been made earlier, naming the individuals appointed and stating that they are present to assist in the conduct of the meeting. The minutes should reflect this.

The substantive body of the minutes should identify each agenda item or issue upon which action was taken. Reports should be recorded, including the name of the presenting member, with a brief summary of the report—unless the report, such as the president's annual report, is contained in other official records of the organization and is therefore accessible from that record. Exhaustive recitation of the financial report is not necessary where financial statements are maintained by the treasurer as an independent permanent record (which should be the case as a matter of good business practice). Where attention is given to a particular part of a report or a financial record, reference to that issue should be made, particularly where attention may be directed to a problem or where an inquiry may invite remedial action. If the content of any report is considered sufficiently important to be made part of the permanent record and no other method of recording the report is readily apparent, the report can be adopted as part of the minutes and attached as an appendix.

Reports and Action Items

Noncontroversial reports may be accepted by the chair and announced "approved as submitted." Such approval, without objection, stands as approval by the meeting. A specific motion for approval, seconded and voted upon, is unnecessary and serves only to waste time and clutter the minutes.

Action items may be introduced by the chair or by a recognized member of the meeting and may be discussed without formal motion. This is particularly appropriate for issues listed in the agenda. Such practice enables the meeting to refine issues or exchange ideas and promotes discovery of ultimate consensus. In fact, experience has shown that in the vast majority of resolved issues, open and informal discussion leads to the natural conclusion of the meeting, which can simply be announced by the chair as the general consensus or sense of the meeting. A statement by the chair to that effect, without objection, is recorded in the minutes and becomes the official decision of the body. This does not mean that every member unequivocally agrees with the conclusion, but that everyone acknowledges the conclusion as the clear sentiment of the majority.

If a general consensus is not apparent, the chair should invite, or any member may offer, a specific motion. The motion becomes the vehicle for ultimate refinement and final statement of the will of the meeting. It need not be preceded by the traditional "whereas" paragraphs if the reason for or appropriateness of the motion is otherwise apparent. Nor must the motion be set apart from the text of the minutes; it may simply be stated within the textual flow. However, if the secretary believes it appropriate to use the more formalistic "whereas" and "be it resolved" format, the practice is not prohibited; it is simply unnecessary in most circumstances. Whether or not the identity of the proposing member or seconding member is noted is within the secretary's discretion. In the record of a final decision, however, should a member desire to note a specific dissent from action taken, and where a roll-call vote is not recorded, the member should be accorded the right of that notation. Otherwise, votes need not be personalized.

At the end of the minutes, it is usually appropriate to announce the date, time, and place of subsequent meetings, if known. The final notation is adjournment by the chair, with or without motion.

TYPICAL MINUTES

CONSOLIDATED TECHNOLOGIES, INC.
ANNUAL MEETING OF SHAREHOLDERS
APRIL 20, 2013

The annual meeting of stockholders of Consolidated Technologies, Inc. was held at the offices of the corporation at 36 Gardner Circle, Pittsburgh, Pennsylvania, on Monday, April 20, 2013, at 10:00 a.m. pursuant to prior written notice to each shareholder.

Robert E. Richardson, board chair, presided and Anita A. Sanders, Esq., vice president—general counsel, was appointed Special Secretary.

The chair called the meeting to order and asked Matthew G. Donnelly, secretary of the corporation, if a quorum was present. Mr. Donnelly stated that proxies had been received representing in excess of 50 percent of the corporation's issued and outstanding stock, thereby constituting a quorum of shareholders under the bylaws of the corporation. The chair announced the meeting duly convened and ready to proceed with its business.

Upon request of the chair, the secretary presented a copy of the notice of the meeting, proxy solicitation materials, and proxy form that had been mailed to each shareholder on March 12, 2013.

The chair announced that, without objection, Gerald P. Underwood, Steven K. Martz, and Joanna E. Carson would serve as tellers and judges of election for the meeting. There being no objection, Mr. Underwood, Mr. Martz, and Ms. Carson were appointed.

The meeting proceeded to the election of seven directors for a one-year term and until their successors are elected and shall qualify to serve. As chair of the nominating committee, Anita A. Sanders stated that in accordance with the bylaws of the corporation, requiring that nominations be submitted at least 14 days prior to the noticed date of the annual meeting, the following nominations had been made: Robert E. Richardson, Arthur L. Anderson, Benjamin L. Eisenberg, Carl J. Coviello, Ruth W. Jensen, John J. Ammonson, and Norman G. Powalski. These nominations had been presented by the nominating committee and approved by the board of directors, and were proposed by management for whom proxy solicitation had been made in connection with call of the meeting. Ms. Sanders announced that the nomination of Troy B. Scott had also been received prior to the nomination closure date and that Mr. Scott's name was also before the meeting as a nominee qualified for election under the corporation's bylaws.

The chair advised that all proxies and any shareholders who

desired to vote in person should cast their ballots with the tellers, and directed the judges to count the ballots.

The chair stated that because a report of operations had been submitted to each shareholder with the proxy solicitation materials, a report would not be given separately at the meeting.

The next item of business was consideration of a proposed amendment to the corporation's articles of incorporation to include a new provision 6(c) to read as follows:

6(c). The shareholders may elect one alternate for each director elected to the board of directors of the corporation. An elected alternate shall serve at any meeting of the board of directors if the director is unable to attend. Nomination and election of alternates shall be subject to requirements for election of directors.

The chair advised that all votes for and against the proposed amendment should be cast with the tellers.

The chair requested that the tellers report the results of voting for directors of the corporation. Mr. Underwood stated that the following votes had been cast:

Name	Votes Cast in Favor
Robert E. Richardson	6,240,212
Arthur L. Anderson	6,240,212

Name	Votes Cast in Favor
Benjamin L. Eisenberg	5,236,120
Carl J. Coviello	5,030,740
Ruth W. Jensen	5,303,740
John J. Ammonson	5,160,260
Norman G. Powalski	5,010,800
Troy B. Scott	16,420

Mr. Underwood announced that as a result of votes cast, Robert E. Richardson, Arthur L. Anderson, Benjamin L. Eisenberg, Carl J. Coviello, Ruth W. Jensen, John J. Ammonson, and Norman G. Powalski were elected the board of directors, to serve until the next annual meeting of the corporation and until their successors are elected and shall qualify.

The chair requested that Mr. Underwood report upon votes cast for and against the proposed amendment to the articles of incorporation. Mr. Underwood responded that 5,016,340 shares had been voted for the proposal and 30,140 shares had been cast against. Thus, the proposal was adopted, and upon filing articles of amendment with the secretary of state, the articles of incorporation will be amended as stated.

The chair inquired whether there were any further matters to come before the meeting. There being none, upon motion seconded and unanimously carried, the meeting was adjourned.

_____/S/_____

Matthew G. Donnelly

TYPICAL BOARD MINUTES

CONSOLIDATED TECHNOLOGIES, INC.
MEETING OF THE BOARD OF DIRECTORS
APRIL 20, 2013

The annual organization meeting of the board of directors of Consolidated Technologies, Inc. was held at the offices of the Corporation, 36 Gardner Circle, Pittsburgh, Pennsylvania, at 10:35 a.m. on Monday, April 20, 2013, pursuant to written notice to each member of the board.

The following board members were present: Robert E. Richardson, Chair of the board; Arthur L. Anderson, president and CEO of the corporation; Benjamin L. Eisenberg; Carl J. Coviello; Ruth W. Jensen; and Norman G. Powalski. Also present were: Bernard H. Wolfson, vice president—Finance; Anita A. Sanders, Esq., Vice president—general counsel; Richard P. Carpenter, vice president—marketing; and Matthew G. Donnelly, secretary of the corporation. Mr. Richardson served as chair of the meeting and Ms. Sanders was appointed special secretary.

The chair announced that a quorum of directors was present and that the meeting, having been duly convened, was ready to proceed with its business. The first item of business was approval of minutes of the previous meeting of January 27, 2013, copies of which had been previously circulated to board members. The chair asked if there were any corrections to the minutes. There being none, the minutes were approved as submitted.

The meeting proceeded to election of officers. Upon motion, seconded and unanimously carried, the following named individuals were elected to the offices set next to their names:

Robert E. Richardson—chair

Arthur L. Anderson—president and CEO

Bernard H. Wolfson—vice president—finance

Anita A. Sanders, Esq.—vice president—general counsel

Richard P. Carpenter—vice president—marketing

Cooper G. Williams—vice president—production

Matthew G. Donnelly—secretary

The chair then proposed election of members to the following committees, who, upon motion, seconded and unanimously carried, were elected to the committees shown:

Executive Committee:

Robert E. Richardson—chair

Arthur L. Anderson

Bernard H. Wolfson

Anita A. Sanders, Esq.

Matthew G. Donnelly

Audit Committee:

Benjamin L. Eisenberg—chair

Ruth W. Jensen

John J. Ammonson

Norman G. Powalski

Finance and Compensation Committee:

Bernard H. Wolfson—chair

Carl J. Coviello

Ruth W. Jensen

John J. Ammonson

Public Relations Committee:

Robert E. Richardson—chair

Arthur L. Anderson

Richard P. Carpenter

Anita A. Sanders, Esq.

Mr. Wolfson reviewed copies of the corporation's financial statements as of December 31, 2012, copies of which had been distributed at the commencement of the meeting. Following Mr. Wolfson's presentation and a brief discussion, the report was accepted as submitted.

Mr. Anderson then delivered the president's report, having distributed beforehand an outline of his presentation with illustrative graphs and schedules. He noted a substantial increase during 2012 for the corporation's telecommunications sector. Whereas revenues in the previous year had been $14.6 million, they had increased to $36.2 million in 2012 chiefly as a result of growth in the graphic telecommunication lines, specifically video conference products, which continue to show a strong potential for growth. He noted, however, that the control sector, featuring principally the company's flow-meter synchro sensors, had turned down during the year to sales of $16.5 million, compared with $19.2 million in 2011. He attributed this reduction to recessive effects of the economy and restrained capital expenditures by domestic high-technology customers. He expressed optimism for the forthcoming year, as a result of not only an expected upturn in the economy but an increased emphasis upon the international market. An extensive discussion followed with respect to the company's usage of agents in the South American market. Mr. Carpenter noted that management's decision last summer to use only exclusive marketing agents had apparently depressed sales since most successful marketers, particularly in Brazil and Argentina, handle several competitive lines. He advised the board that the management had recently made the decision to discontinue the policy of using only dedicated, exclusive agents. Mr. Anderson reported that company employment in manufacturing had increased from 540 to 627 full-time employees over the last quarter, an increase attributable to new manufacturing requirements for telecommunications equipment. Mr. Anderson called upon Mr. Wolfson to report on a proposed amendment to the company's incentive savings plan.

Mr. Wolfson distributed an outline of the current incentive savings plan, together with a proposed change to the company's contribution percentage as well as a proposal to lessen required vesting time. Mr. Wolfson reported that during the calendar years 1990 and 1991 there had been a small but steady decline of employee participation in the plan, something previously believed to be a product of economic conditions. However, as a result of an employee survey conducted in January, he discovered general perceptions that employees considered (1) the company's 25 percent matching contribution to be insufficient as a savings incentive and (2) the five-year vesting period to be too long. As set forth in the distributed proposal for revision, Mr. Wolfson suggested an increase of the company's matching contribution to 35 percent and a reduction of vesting time from five years to three years. Following discussion, it was moved, seconded, and unanimously carried that management's recommendation be accepted, increasing the company's matching contribution to 35 percent and reducing participant vesting from five years to three years.

As unfinished business, the chair requested that Ms. Sanders report upon negotiations for a continued lease of the company's storage facility at Greenwood Industrial Park in Somerset, Pennsylvania. Ms. Sanders advised that the Company had signed a three-year lease extension upon the same terms and conditions as under the prior lease, except that the owner had agreed to remove escalation provisions that management and the board had considered troublesome because of their open-ended nature. Ms. Sanders advised that those provisions have been deleted and that an extension of the lease had been signed by management but was made contingent upon board approval. Following brief discussion, Ms. Sanders was commended for a very positive negotiation, and it was the sense of the meeting that the lease extension be approved as proposed.

Mr. Richardson asked if there was new business to come before the meeting. There being none, he announced that the next meeting would be held in July and that notice of time and date would be circulated in early June. The chair then adjourned the meeting.

__/s/_____

Matthew G. Donnelly, secretary

Index